The Icon Effect

The Icon Effect

Sloane Montgomery

CONTENTS

1 | Introduction 1

2 | Historical Icons 5

3 | Cultural Icons 11

4 | Political Icons 17

5 | Entertainment Icons 23

6 | Business Icons 29

7 | The Psychology of Iconography 35

8 | The Icon Effect on Society 37

9 | Conclusion 39

1

Introduction

Famous figures—politicians, movie stars, authors, and humanitarians—shape our world in outsized ways. Physicists posit that for every action, there's an equal and opposite reaction, and we might make a similar case for celebrity. Contemporary psychotherapists argue that in our mediation-saturated world, driven in part by a numbing array of digital stimuli, dissociation, rather than repression, is most likely what characterizes depression and "melancholia" in the 21st century. For those at risk for depression, living more and more vicariously is significantly less satisfying than the thrilling characters streaming through our luminous screens.

In this book, we want to spend a little time working through what we call The Icon Effect. Icons shape individuals and societies in deep ways—peoples, tribes, and civilizations have grouped around and coalesced energy toward icons from the beginning of time. But icons do not necessarily evoke happiness or positive outcomes. Many religions have warned about setting up false gods or worshiping idols. Those warnings likely emerged from the earliest human knowledge and have been recast through different stories and traditions for generations.

We suggest there are two types of icons—pathological and heroic icons—and as a civilization, we routinely seek to find a balance between them. Since icons are created according to collective agreements or consensual hallucinations, as long as the culture is strong and unified, this can be achieved—especially around pathological icons that have served useful purposes. Those pathological icons are contrary to health, but no less important than heroic ones—in fact, they are often harbingers of a coming crisis and an opportunity for the culture to grow, evolve, and mature. Let's explore The Icon Effect further.

Defining Icons

The word "icon," when applied to people, is by far the most slippery of terms. To apply it with precision, then, we will have to narrow it down, and we can do that by analyzing how the term is presently used. The characteristic of icons is the very passage from being just a figure or a celebrity to being someone who has, in the most diverse of areas, imposed the mark of their own time or is capable of remaining beyond the time they dominated. Simultaneously, an icon touches us personally, without our being able to say why. This is what is truly marvelous about it! They impress us without immediate reason, by a mysterious transfer of their charisma. Their face is in the first stages of transubstantiation, becoming a "mask" behind which an indescribable hypostasis is lovingly entertained. The name of the icon is also known by the enemies who are beyond good and evil, and it seems improbable that one could be apathetically indifferent to them. Icons, then, almost automatically provoke an opinion, divided between those who adore and worship them perhaps with too much fervor.

Icons do not emerge but are made. They are not wholly imagined, yet they are more than real. They require public opinion, and frequent "milestone" events can provide them with a mirror. These "mirrors" are exceptional events that act as investment musicians, thus contributing to mosaicist popularity. The icons have an accentuated presence, even when they die. They live virtuality for the community that been molded by the subjects regarding the art: they do not need to "be," or in any case to "resemble" anything, they suffice to represent themselves in their own collective potentiality. They will have already made the lyricists to their nature in motion—the former gods, among them, to follow.

The Power of Influence

It cannot be denied that Diana Spencer was an exceptional person who had come to embody all the hopes of the British monarchy, emerging as a major public personage in the process. Her legend has transcended her and lives on long afterwards, which might prompt us to look more closely at Un Génie du Marketing.

What impact do famous figures have, and why do they have it? Icons embody not skills, but values; not qualities, but systems of reference; not behavior, but ethics. Idols are living proof that, in a rapidly changing world, anything – and certainly not talent, of which only ephemeral expression may exist – can be replaced. The skill and devotion of a Madonna, a Zidane or a Jobs have nothing to do with it; nor is it, as Virginia Postrel suggests in an imprecise fashion, a "subtle alchemy of good taste, conscientiousness and hard work". At any rate, the obsession with discovering the recipe that supposedly made these figures must be interpreted in and of itself. Logic is a dream dialectic that constructs its reality through a series of ramified logico-semantic filters. Society is not built with objective facts, but out of a narrative and a vision, whatever that might be. So, populist "idolatry" appears as a profound misunderstanding of this logic.

2 |

Historical Icons

Ancient: Kings, Monks, and Clever Men 1. Gilgamesh. 5000 years ago. 2. Caesar Augustus. 2,000 years ago. 3. St. Augustine: 1600 years ago.

Medieval: Prophets & Warriors 1. Jesus Christ: 1,500 years ago. 2. King Arthur: 800 years ago. 3. Genghis Khan: 800 years ago.

Modern: Kings, Scientists, and an Actor 1. Martin Luther and the German Peasants' War: 450 years ago. 2. Isaac Newton. 300 years ago. 3. Goethe (or Napoleon). 250 years ago. 4. William Shakespeare. 400 years ago.

Icons in Our World Most people have disparate networks where a few hubs have many connections (long-tail networks), but others (of which they are not a part) have relatively few. That's what gives networks their structure and is one reason why tipping points happen. In determining who these few hubs are, we may have selected people (or, occasionally, institutions) from all walks of life. And, indeed, we can think of hubs as many giants of history, some we hold up as admirable examples and others we despise. We've been writing a book called "The Icon Effect: Why Some Figures Matter More than Others" to examine whether or not these recurring iconic figures from across time differ from the rest of us mere mortals, and, if they do, in what ways. And, not least, whether the factors that make them iconic have seen any changes as we have moved from an agrarian to an industrial and then a digital society.

Ancient Icons

Almost every civilization in antiquity had people that were considered "iconic." This title denoted that these figures had a lasting and profound impact on the socio-political fabric of their time and their achievements were memorialized in every field of human endeavor, be it the arts, religion, or intellectual thought. They were important not just for what they did, but for what they could potentially bestow on others. The "powers" of these iconic figures spanned a vast array of possible human desires, usually connected in some way to fame, wealth, political power, or safety.

In ancient Egypt, writing letters to famous figures to intercede on one's behalf was a well-established practice, a practice that continued straight through to the end of the Roman period. Although the advent of Christianity effectively rendered the old gods and goddesses of ancient Egypt defunct, one aspect of them continued to live on in spirit at least. For even in an ancien regime was brought down and a monolithic new belief system—one that painted the old Pharaonic ways as heretical and unacceptable—was instituted, the oracles that had rooted their knowledge in Isis remained both popular and important. These contrived figures, which purported to be channeling knowledge from the otherworld, became the new conduits by which people could connect with the ancient gods and also—the unseen deliberate irony of the ancient texts translate well here—the ancient kings and queens of Egypt who had just been roundly condemned by the new god, God "in and of Jesus Christ".

Medieval Icons

The word "icon" literally means that which looks like something else, and during the medieval period in the Byzantine Empire, the religious icons of Jesus, the Virgin Mary, and the saints played a major role in how Europeans saw their culture, their society, and the universe. While the Popes were supposed by Christian theology to be the stewards of Christ's vision on earth, in practice popular devotion was often centered around images. Just ask the priest who begrudgingly pulled a St. Walfrid banner rally its constituents from the Pew! The power of icons in the medieval mindset is something J.R.R. Tolkien may have been reaching for when he saw fit to have a witch outsmart one of the most powerful, if not the most powerful, devil of them all by putting him in a position where he cannot see the world as he wishes it was; she turned his own powers of illusion against him. Thus, the icon ceases to represent the real organisms or forces which it personifies and takes on an identity all its own. This is especially the case when icons are being treated as images, such as painting, especially if they are being painted of give it subject matter, such as the divine.

In the minds of medieval peasants the protagonists of their religious dramas enjoyed pride of place in the culture of their day, a place that has been left vacant by modern men. For medieval man, Jesus, Mary, the saints, and even the devils, weren't so much ideals as they were ancestors. When a medieval peasant prayed to the Virgin Mary to intercede for him, he wasn't just putting in a word with the Godhead, by whom, as one common salvation-hopeful put it, the Virgin Mary holds her status as the ultimate parole officer. Every time a medieval peasant farmer knelt and opened his heart in prayer to the Virgin Mary- every time that he felt he was sharing a moment privy communication - he was doing so with someone he imagined he knew. The traditional Christian icon is usually a painting of Jesus, the Virgin Mary, or the Saints, and the icon's spiritual function is to act as either a psychological stimulus or as an actual recipient or container within which the divine repose majestically. It is because the power of the divine is radiation outwards into the icon, or because man's intensity of admiration and yearning for the divine is so great that it may be poured into the icon.

Modern Icons

Modern icons are arguably the most powerful speakers of the 'brand' metaphor, as they have the power to beam images and values far beyond national borders. One of the best-known current figures, Nelson Mandela, epitomizes the meld of political activism and philanthropy. After forty-six years in jail, he emerged to lead his country to racial unity and becoming the first black president of South Africa. His wearing of an AIDS ribbon at the 46664 concert in his honor was as iconic as his election. Another political icon is Aung San Suu Kyi, who, while under house arrest, led her political party to victory in 1990 only to see that victory reversed by the ruling military. She was awarded the Nobel Peace Prize in 1991 and has become an icon in the struggle for Myanmar/Burma's release from dictatorship. The third political figure who has brought iconic status to herself has been US Secretary of State Condoleezza Rice: her ability to transcend race and gender is aimed at inspiring individuals across the globe.

The Antarctic ecoexplorer, Robert Swan, has vowed to 'walk young people to the end of the earth to see if they love it enough to save it'. A parka and sunglasses is as much his uniform as a dyspeptic Stowe arguing for a moratorium on radicalism. Another iconic ecoexplorer is the first person to have traversed the four major deserts of the world, Australian Brigitte Muir. She developed a sense of moral responsibility in individuals. Pope John Paul II played a significant role in the fall of Communism, particularly his much-quoted statement: 'The human person is the way of the Church.' The Virgin Mart is an unlikely contemporary icon. The president of a transnational ad agency likened Richard Branson in November 2005 to an undersized Rambo, a 'sauvegardeur' whose daredevil cuteness and predilection for circus stunts was the force behind Virgin Blue in Australia and Virgin Express in Belgium.

3 |

Cultural Icons

One of the top-selling Lithuanian writers, Jurga Ivanauskaitė, claimed to follow her own interests, not the will of the masses: 'I would never write a book for a bestseller. I am privileged not to have to do this'. However, the high sales of her literary works seemed paradoxical. In a world heavily saturated with different literary, artistic, and musical works, both by popular and underground creators, what makes people read literary Nobel Prize laureates, empathize with their beloved Dickens characters, admire Van Gogh paintings, listen to Bach or Madonna? In this paper, we provide examples from literature, art, and music and dissect those figures that are admired by many. Scholars align cultural icons with those who themselves shape their respective art and/or challenge society, thereby generating new art, setting new trends, or shaping worldview. Cultural icons are often characterized by a large following which often consists of members of diverse backgrounds, general society. The influence of the iconic persona or work is subtle and varied. Not only does the iconic individual himself influence the direction of artistic expression, he also influences other values and societal movements.

Cultural icons help inspire need creativity by embodying it in words, sound, picture, composition. Cultural icons are admired by some, respectfully critiqued by others; they shape the worldview of both creators and 'regular' people—i.e., they shape our world. The cultural icon drew inspiration from various Western, ancient, and classical literatures and mythologies, religions, and hallowed events. This inspiration has a contemporary aesthetic significance other than providing mere spectacle. The icon's work often has a visionary component, which ties in with the explosion, capabilities, and potential of the creative individual, resulting in a variety of social and personal commentaries. When the everyday and everyone had meaning, the iconic gesture, and iconic work rise above all, initializing change.

Literary Icons

The possibility of belonging to the gallery of authors who have achieved and retained for centuries the seal of iconic weight is, initially, a bit intimidating. Yet, all writers are potentially iconic, or have had a brush with their own iconography. On a deeper level, to be an iconoclast is to seek to be godlike oneself, to summon a world between the lines that will endure, parallel men and their critiquing tongues. Even if ignored or misunderstood during the author's lifetime and beyond, even if the illusion is that the iconoclasm practiced its own author by doom and backlash. Sometimes part of this iconography, as practice and symbolism, becomes part of the author's fiction and nonfiction itself—a metaiconization of one's own work, a transcendent disguise and purpose.

In common conversation, an icon can be identified not by physical or literal evidence, just as an author does not necessarily need to be physically dead to be iconic. History bulks the ravaged shelf-tree of culture with a lot of dead icons; literary iconicity speaks to a dimension of shared culture and intellectual thought. These figures tell readers, and are told by readers, what "literature" has already said and can say. These distinguished men and women are long-stand-ing guests of our mental rooms of thought, spinning, as Eliothen describes Dante's Beatrice, the air that one is breathing. They frequently veil Nadine Gordimer's "more noise than signal," telling us of a world in an author's work that, living, we may not wish to come near.

Artistic Icons

In the art world, artistic icons represent a milestone. Their influence can be seen in the work of contemporary, yet unknown, artists. Van Gogh's influence was so pervasive that even a modern artist who was not trying to recreate his style was referred to other artists' work by being told that it looked like some derivative of his work. The other artist did not mean it as a compliment but saw nothing else to compare it to. Michelangelo's talents instigated movements from his immediate followers of Mannerism in the fourteenth century to the Mannerists and Caravaggisti in Italy in 1600. His followers traveled to France and offered the Jean Mouret boys an alternative training in sculpture. The Bramantists continued to pursue and promote the elegance of linear designs while the Michelangelesque joined the Venetian to focus on color and forms beneath the figures, for instance.

Picasso's movie "Sylvette" was plastered with Pablo's image. He purchased an old beach town where he built and lived in a new studio. With Sylvette in tow, he commuted for six months to Albert, France, to produce some 17 paintings, ensembles, drawings, and small ceramics which would affect an architectural innovation in Cubism. Art Movements: Braque moved south to L'Estaque after the war. The village had been a hotspot for Cezanne, and the man even moved there for just a few short years until he was run off by the local fruit peddlers who traded their wares at the same site of this now famous old house art museum. Two years earlier, Georges

Braque painted The Harbor at L'Estaque. Today the 20' x 25' painting has been housed in Amsterdam's Vincent Van Gogh Art Museum. Throughout art history, artists clumped together to brainstorm, collaborate, inspire, and compete. The Old Guard, as the media coined them, got headwise advice from Gertrude Stein as Robert Frank attempted to overtake them in the fifties. Little did we know at the time that these artists would all share the same title, genius.

Musical Icons

Music, just as is the case with every other art form, is not only susceptible to the power of iconic figures but is often mostly shaped and sometimes even completely informed by them. Some people, Singer writes, are not only the best at what they do, but possess a certain quality that ensures that 'what they do becomes the standard by which others are judged'. What is the power of a great musician? A musician can give birth to an entirely new musical genre, thus informing the evolution of a domain much larger than artistic culture. The reggae musician Bob Marley, for instance, did not only make reggae music popular. He created and shaped reggae to such an extent that 'Bob Marley's name would forever be inextricably entrapped within both the history and the carriage of reggae'.

The power of a great musician, however, is not confined to the shaping of musical genres - an icon has the power to embody a complete epoch, to stand as the very symbol of that age. It is difficult to take, for example, to relate the elusive, free-spirited pursuit of hedonistic pleasure of the Jazz Age without the invocation of the era's grand icon, Scott Fitzgerald's memorable figure, Jay Gatsby, or the world-weary glamour of Paris, France without mention of her timeless twin icons Hemingway and Fitzgerald. Similarly, in other parts of the world, the Italian Renaissance is not only the name of a historical period, but denotes a specific cultural style, all of which centers on another of history's myriad iconic figures, Michelangelo. While no one would claim that these writers or artists are the "cause" of a certain historical or cultural development, historical specie cannot overlook their importance as archetypal figures. It is less plausibly, one need not appeal to band histories and cultural records properly to appreciate the power of a great musician. Having been formed in Heidelberg, a location known reverently as 'the center of morally decrepit university carousals', the author has often had to resist hearty rounds of cheap German ale while partying to a live traditional band, whose rock and roll performances consist mostly of covers of the Rolling Stones, Elvis, and Bob Marley. Cultural osmosis is a marvelous and often subconscious process, for most German youth who love the Three Kinds of Icon were probably not even alive when all three musicians stopped playing live concerts. This is a world of Janet Malcolm's representative way of looking: 'a microscope with a cause'. In essence, there is a large community which has not only had their musical tastes, but the entire ethos which underlines their approach to Western popular culture, shaped by these three musicians signing such less often-heard tunes as "Let it Bleed" and "The Sun Don't Shine". There is an addiction to Bob, though most of our Three Kings of Icon may often not realize it. So much of our personal and popular culture, our 'cast of mind', was impregnated and borne by such artists, and passed down to us. It is a point to remember, living in a land that advertises itself as a meritocracy, that a song can be passed down from generation to generation and inform all of us more about the era in which we live than a faceful of MTV-graphed images of our most popular musical figures.

4 |

Political Icons

There are three categories of political figures or groups that have the potential to constitute political icons: revolutionary leaders such as Ayatollah Khomeini, Mao Tse Tung, Sandinistas, Sinn Fein, Fidel Castro, Nelson Mandela, Pol Pot, Jean-Bertrand Aristide, and Maoists; presidents and prime ministers (and imperial leaders) such as Margaret Thatcher, Clement Attlee, John F. Kennedy, Tony Blair, Franklin Delano Roosevelt, Sir Winston Churchill, Ronald Reagan, Major Coleman, General de Gaulle, Charles de Gaulle, Sergeant Maj Corps, Helmut Kohl, Joseph Stalin, Mikhail Gorbachev, Otto Von Bismarck, Harry Truman, Carlsberg, George Bush, Abraham Lincoln, David Ben Gurion, Johannes Vorster, Lee Kwan Yew, Indira Gandhi, Ataturk, Adolf Hitler, Josef Stalin, Selwyn Lloyd, Harold Wilson, Haile Selassie, John Smith, Francois Mitterrand, Herbert Lieberman, Oliver Cromwell, Ivan the Terrible, Ramses the Great, King Canute, Prince Valium, Joshua Nkomo, Kang Chu, Ratu Charles Korber, Marquess of Salisbury, Isoroku Yamamoto, John Foster Dulles, and Marshal Applewhite; and activists/humanitarians such as Joy Adamson, Sister Theresa, Mohandas Karamchand (Mahatma) Gandhi, and Princess Diana whose humanity and vision have directly or indirectly influenced policy and/or belief in virtually all governments and societies on the planet.

Protests and war, the environment and human rights have been inspired by and fought about in the name of political icons. Complaints, reforms, and policies from the land issue in pre-revolution South Africa to British and Israel's attitude to Palestine to the war in Iraq and the regulation of the international banking system have been shaped by contemporary leaders and prime ministers and in many cases by what those who have deposed and succeeded them or govern despite them do or say. It may not be overstating the case to suggest that it is the political icons—the towering giants that have been leaders of national movements, countries, or international governing/coordinated bodies.

Revolutionary Leaders

Revolutionary leaders are the George Washingtons and Mao Zedongs, the Simón Bolívars and Maximilien Robespierres: they embody the revolution. Prior to their rise, the conditions and causes of the coming revolution have been developing for decades, and will continue functioning even after the leader has been deposed or dead for years. Nevertheless, the leader is the lynchpin of the revolution. This idea, a new approach to the study of the phenomenon, offers a clear and useful structure as well as casts new light on the process of revolution. It should not be surprising that leaders of all kinds have been ignored in studies of revolution. After all, followers comprise about 99% of any mass. Followers are more important than leaders in mass movements for the same reason that shares of corporate stock are worth more than convertible debentures. When Khrushchev and Nixon met in 1959 to debate the relative merits of capitalism and communism, the contest quickly focused on who the working class liked better. In this scenario, the key question is how a follower becomes a leader.

Not every revolution has a single leader, of course. The American Revolution had factions but not the single leader that Lenin implanted in the concept. The French Revolution had several, none more important than Robespierre, but no Northern Star that the whole country pursued as inexorably as the one the Bolsheviks hunted. Artistic incompatibilities tore asunder the revolutionary leadership in Russia, causing Lenin to have executives who were as worthless as Robespierre, the man who until then had fascinated him. Even more rare is the revolution with a leadership oligarchy, a group that is not always unanimous but that always can force agreement on the most important matters. The Chinese Revolution is the prime example of the oligarchical revolution.

Presidents and Prime Ministers

Presidents and prime ministers shape our world as governance continues to concentrate into presidencies or prime ministerships. Even when they don't have direct power, their quite precarious work can define not only domestic policy making, but also give a unique gloss to an entire era of global policy development. Consider President Donald Trump, who brought the perils of crude power maximization back to U.S. foreign policy and so shook strategic systems the world over. Or Hungarian Prime Minister Viktor Orbán, who, despite the recent shrunken parliamentary majority, has done more than anyone else to change the politics of managing governance since 2010.

Presidents and prime ministers aren't merely managers. With nuclear codes at their fingertips or at the cutting edge of largely untrammeled Indian Ocean delimitation practices, the chances of things going very wrong and very right seem to be increasing each year. The last U.S. president with a broad shadow beyond his term was, of course, Harry Truman, whose meta-geoeconomic ties to the post-

World War II era made his foreign policies inviolate and unspeakable, despite his numerous policy failures. Even now, as Mr. Truman's legacy is open for reassessment, President Joe Biden is an heir to Mr. Truman's ordained internationalism. Go to any region of the world and you can still find parts of diplomacy and governance laid in his image. In Israel, America itself has suddenly become an image of Mr. Biden, much as the Egypt of the 1950s came to embody the image of President Dwight Eisenhower.

Activists and Humanitarians

One last area of significant contribution to humanity is in activists and humanitarians. Many of the social issues which we face are due to deeply held societal mindsets and a suffusing belief that certain people are "less than" and deserve less, whether they are the poor, animals, criminals, those of other races or ethnicities, children, etc. Many of those who are changing those mindsets are doing so through education and showing people a better way to live and treat their fellow creatures. Several of the few ideologies respected and socially ingratiated with the Founding Fathers' wisdom include their belief in a separation of church and state and their belief in the equal rights of all living beings.

Consequently, one of the longest-running and most successful groups of humanitarians the earth has seen is animal rights. Henry VIII of England released millions of serfs and provided legislation in the form of the Statute of Artificers. The impersonal legal liberation of slaves was even embedded in the laws of Hammurabi. In contrast, though the earth has mainly been a place where the strong and powerful dominate the weak and less powerful, earth history has shown that while the rights of people are pressured and minimized for long durations of time, occasionally a liberator appears, and those few humanitarians tirelessly claw us from the trogloditic shells of our sadistic barbarians to an enlightened society of respect and dignity. Such advocates of human rights are also lauded yet still reviled. Their approach to humans is as varied as the people whose cases they champion for an ideal society. Some fight for prisoners in war, others for runaways, others for religious persuasion, and still others for the immoralized criminals who sprout such peculiar, psychotic flowers as murder, rape, abuse, and torture. Some focus on those who are habitually disregarded, as in the tired, poor, et cetera et cetera, while others focus on educating society about the mental and psychological differences between themselves and non-abusers. The humanitarian's lack of compassion can be an educational tool meant to make us more sensitive to morality because it contrasts with what is widely accepted; thus it gives us headlines to be pious about. Among such humanitarians and activists, as with any other group, there will also be those individuals whose victims were known solely to those of a particularly narrow demographic, such as Anna Dickinson, Elizabeth Blackwell, and Sojourner Truth (women's rights in the nineteenth century) and hundreds more charismatic leaders who made the front page of The Hampshire Chronicle.

Entertainment Icons

Film and television stars are some of the most prolific icons in the world. Think of a person everyone knows. More than likely, someone made famous by movies and TV is where you want to start. Leonardo DiCaprio, The Beatles, Marie Osmond, and Malala Yousafzai have all had a massive popular impact and changed the world in some way. Others, such as Elvis, Audrey Hepburn, Heath Ledger, and Meghan Markle, may be public figures performing a role, and their iconic status is transferred by performance.

Sports. Quite simply, everyone knows Elvis and Muhammad Ali, Michael Jordan, and Babe Ruth. Tiger Woods, Tiger King, Maria Sharapova, Earvin Prince, Peter Norman, Daniel Sturridge, and the Georgia Tech swim team. Athletic ability is not the only reason someone could unlock a pedestal in this calabash. Influence is not about power, nor is it about priority. Mira Nair directed "Queen of Katwe" and gathered kids from the streets of Katwe to develop a legacy of enthusiasm and travel with their local chess coach from slum to slum. Icons from sport dominate the fashion and music world, have a globally worshipped cult compound, and can command global flash publicity as a DJ. It is already the internet age, of course, and digital signs have been released. For the past two decades, we have yet referred to the ones we now recognize as the "instafamous" or "twelebrity" or "YouTuber". Some, such as Kim Kardashian's "selfies", have released iconic images that label the thing they document. Social media icons reflect popular culture with a dazzle and negotiate an identity, and losers are currencies on the internet where social media cues are placed there for us and played out. They also innovate as computers to create and foster digital escalates of real life, such as FKA twigs' "Pole Dancer" routine and Greenpeace's "#PigLeaks" robocalls to Christmas hypermarkets. Social media publicity generates unrest, raises political awareness, enforces the refugee asylum case, and makes sports licensing a breakthrough.

Film and Television Stars

The major stars of film and television remain iconic figures – even in death. The likes of Greta Garbo, James Stewart, and Marilyn Monroe continue to fascinate us whether in festivals and revivals, books, or galleries. Sometimes their films are remade. Here the new stars get to express their allegiance to their illustrious predecessors and shine brightly just for a little while. Their reputations then return to the shadow of those whose shoes they briefly filled. All these stars and many others are subject to trivia quizzes and recreations of their most famous performances. Their lines have, of course, made their way into everyday language. 'Wherever shall I find my ambition now?' and 'I'll be back' are common enough across three generations of theatergoers. And they appear in every vernacular.

However, film and television matter not only as works of art and entertainment but also as news, debate, educational resources, industrial output, and part of our visual heritage. The first reports of film arrivals or unique screenings expressed the new significance of the form, as did those making their claim for films as an art form. The earliest press reports tended to ignore the films in favor of the Lumière Brothers who would soon become vague historical figures themselves. As the genius for building a business empire, Walt Disney emerged, he and Mickey Mouse owed much to the activities of flesh and blood Disney and his enduring musical talents. Today Disney continues to be strongly associated with the star power of various animators, singers, dancers, actresses turned media corp, though they are waging a strong campaign to pivot towards Disney the brand/culture artifact. In 2007, of course, Apple aligned itself with Bono and U2 and, in 2015, we also have Apple's new friend, Taylor Swift, taking on Spotify and its peers.

Sports Icons

The world of sport belongs to an elite few, providing them accolades, adulation, and influence over billions of fans. A glimpse of irony, often referred to as the "sporting gods" legend, the allure of what these few regular people are able to accomplish is often beyond comprehension. Whether it's the mystical talent of Lionel Messi and Sir Donald Bradman or the inspiring stories of someone prevailing against all possible odds like Oprah Winfrey or Michael Jordan, these sporting icons have an emissive allure that compels the world to watch on in awe. Their abilities alter the competitive landscape in sports so radically that the proceedings and outcomes cease to be matters of global products of sports leagues and organizations and instead are molded into the fates of these singular individuals.

The impact of sports icons, however, does not end at the borders of the sports field or industry. Throughout the history of sport's existence, its icons have helped inspire generations of athletes and brought billions of fans into the fold of global sporting fandom. The international reach and consumption of sports rests heavily on presenting a transcendent admirability and an emotional magnetism of competitive action. Building the iconicity of an individual is crucial to building the global value of a sports league, team, or event. Enacting international appeal to stimulate global interest in a sport has included icons like David Beckham's fashion savvy, Lewis Hamilton's swaggering ego, and Michael Jordan's ruthless competitiveness. All these traits and others build out the mythology of an international superstar and help in the global reproduction of images, coverage, and stories of these global influencers.

Internet Influencers

What is the true nature of an icon? A mirror reflecting the collective dreams, society's fears, and aspirations? Are they fetishes or ideals frozen in a timeless present? One thing is certain: apart from history's only objective reflection of what occurs at a specific time and place, it matters little whether they're famous for being famous or famous for being a poet or philosopher. The vitiated concept of an icon sewn into some eras imposes a kind of moral residue on them by forcing them into a role of political victim, cultural fatalist, or 'court jester' who says one thing and does another. How are we to understand the untouchable autocrats of meaning of the classic magazines that have passed not from blood to blood according to some Byzantine or medieval genealogy, but from the cold fingers of one publishing magnate to another?

In the digital age, a kind of new clique of trends has been on the rise over the last 20 years; we're talking, of course, about the internet influencers. The brands, and the professionals working within them, have correspondingly rebranded them as "content creators who use social media to promote their projects and communicate with their fans," for a better mission-appropriate lexicon. The internet has shifted the scale of wisdom, fame, and power from the hallowed and untouchable into the regime of the fragile and fleeting. Swiftly, the transitory "superior pedigrees" of the digital space were overwrought with memes and the icons, some of whom now have popular juices, boasting tens of millions of dollars and their own beauty lines. They couldn't care less; we guess this desire to be larger-than-life, in principle, remains the same today.

6 |

Business Icons

I t's difficult for investors to capture the same outsize returns from their high-conviction trades that greatly improve their portfolios over the long term. Some influential figures help to buck that trend and have an outsize impact on both industries and economies. We've identified over 30 such individuals across business, investing, media, and politics. This is a deeper dive on the effect that some major business leaders have had on the business world. The business icons we chose have met certain criteria: they helped to innovate a new technology or were CEOs at companies where research and development was crucial and helped to drive innovation in a variety of sectors. We also included entrepreneurs who are changing industry trends, not just in tech. Although Jeff Bezos may have a significant impact on the future of retail through Amazon.com Inc. (AMZN), Elon Musk strives to make his business icons powerful enough to be taken seriously. We broke down our business icons further into three categories: tech innovators, entrepreneurs, and corporate leaders.

Two hundred years of economic history suggest that industrial revolutions come in waves. The First Industrial Revolution was powered by coal, the Second by electricity, and the Third by computing. Now, business leaders are harnessing a wave of "technological" breakthroughs — including machine learning, robotics, drone technology, augmented reality, and 3-D printing — to make what amounts to a Fourth Industrial Revolution. They're using these trends to reshape the way people work, live, and interact. Business leaders are on the front lines of this new, Fourth Industrial wave, and they come in all forms. They are entrepreneurs tapping technology to create new companies, and corporate leaders — the business icons in the industrial revolution — at large businesses striving to make better use of a $2.4 trillion information technology sector. These businessmen are using a variety of tactics to administer change. For one, they're upscaling their workforces and finding the employees sorely needed to make the 14-million-person information-technology industry tick. And they're investing in the technological change itself. These business leaders make decisions that have outsized effects on the industries in the world today.

Tech Innovators

In the fifth issue of "The Icon Effect," we look past the trappings of Silicon Valley hipness and dive into the tech innovators who have fully arrived and now shape the world we live in: Tech Innovators. Their products and platforms are our constant companions in work, shopping, and socializing - and they have also fostered a good deal of technological disruption. Tech innovators now lead over a third of the companies in the Nasdaq. When tech innovators go public, they offer extreme guidance of their companies' future direction and advise Wall Street on where society is headed. Their books and memoirs also guide us throughout the digital transformation. Some of their more transformative ideas include societal and environmental issues. Innovators are busy building and creating digital infrastructures, in doing so are becoming more political in their careful rebranding of mission statements and engineering narratives.

Tech innovators transform calculus. Kodak, BlackBerry, Zoom and Biogen convince us that shortcuts to financial significance involve plastic cameras, wireless email, video calls and quantum computing has taken root in pop culture. Indeed, the rise of tech innovators has long been a trope of American entrepreneurship and emblematic of the Ivanpah solar plant. But it also can be damned by tech titan launch failure and the pop culture moniker "folksagemaker" and "folksawfulsiliconhollow" and "techcreaminafieldofapples." The volatility underscores the sociotechnological reality, which, investment speculation aside, has flourished under the recent product and platform engineering leadership of some innovators and the authoritative global culture. Judging from many stratified metrics, tech innovators have begun to satisfy an enduring elite stamp.

Entrepreneurs

Entrepreneurs have always had a special place in American culture. They're seen as hardworking, passionate innovators and visionaries, dedicated to furthering their business ventures and building startups into large, successful enterprises. But what causes us to see many of these figures as iconic? What makes some individuals in business into symbols of their industry? Entrepreneurial icons are enduring in their influence, yet there is currently little understanding of how some figures become iconic in the contemporary imagination.

The figure of the entrepreneur is a globally recognized symbol for the vibrancy of national economies and the excesses of capitalism. Americans have long valued entrepreneurial figures as cultural markers of innovation and economic progress, famous for their work to improve lives and drive economies. We have worked to enumerate their contributions to industrial organization and business strategy. Knowing what we do from this tripartite analysis of entrepreneurship literature, the entrepreneur can be seen as the face of an industry, the strategy and motivation of the company, and the foundational theory for the economy's productive power. By breaking cultural representations down into themes and patterns, the curious reader can begin to understand basic differences in the icon effect between the civil engineer and the cowboy, or the problems inherent in becoming iconic for new and smaller industry.

Corporate Leaders

As long-established captains of industry fade into the background, large listed companies have noticed exciting possibilities on their coattails. The emphasis on leaders is not only beneficial for their own long-term career prospects, but it also complements the management philosophy of many "icon firm" executives. Organizational expert Gareth Jones suggests that while "a leader may have a significant impact and support the company's strategy, markets, culture, and behavior," corporate leaders also affect other organizational dynamics over time. "Even after they have left the business," the gap between leaders does not entirely disappear, says Jones. As has been pointed out, leaders can envisage different organizational roles and structures through their commitment to certain cultural and social aspects with the aim of incorporating them into particular ideologies.

Jones poses the concern of what happens if you become an "icon leader" and believes that it could be concluded that "who you are as a person has as much impact as what you do as a leader." So what builds an organization with an iconic market position or an iconic city? Among the potential solutions, such as training and public relations. The very obvious aspects of becoming an organizational legend are what make being present as a leader so difficult for its members. Leaders are deemed to have extraordinary powers, thereby "underpinning the greater power of these folios who create a picture of the universe." Influences are also increasingly downloaded on titanium dimensions.

7

The Psychology of
Iconography

When opting for icons as the subject of research, one might think of them in psychological terms, that is, as mediators shaping our perceptions and creating emotions of the kind Habermas called "aesthetic" - emotions through which one binds herself emotionally to her fellow citizens. Many researchers in the area of iconography may in fact be using the term icon as a node in order to discuss the hegemonic and ethical aspects of their referential subjects or the aesthetic and moral experience of those who look at icons. Critical thinking according to Morozov investigates the rationality of many aspects of everyday reality. The present paper takes a different path: Equating icons and media celebrities, if an authentic effect is enacted by their means, the need that arises may involve retracing how, concretely, this happens. If we do so, we find a rich vein in the twists and turns of psychological research on the powerful effect of iconic figures. Of course, in 1971 Gabriele Amorth, the then leader of the Vatican's exorcism unit, knew this: "Collective, cross-ethnic experiences of World Wars and atrocities have been somehow assimilated. [Witnesses and survivors] have borne some sort of intrapsychic profit for themselves and for society" (cited in Danziger, 1997, p. 27).

This "fundamental (in)justice" insufflates us with emotions: Socrates calls it timê, the Protestant Reformation sees it as an inner presence of the divine Word, Carl Schmitt names it "miracle" and "Grace," Habermas speaks of a disruptive, inexplicable "aesthetic experience", a "primordial... and contentious form of cognition" that is "prediscursive," to be investigated by social psychology, a term that means "before the acquisition of language" and refers to the sets of rules and expectations constituting a communicative community prior to conscious, explicit agreement.

The Icon Effect on Society

Erica James, Murat Kristal, Sheena Iyengar (2021) address the subject of the influence of the most famous figures on society in all domains of activity and from different perspectives. They analyze the dynamics of the evolution and representation of icons in society, touching upon such topics as the branding of personalities, the hierarchy among the most famous people, and the priming effect of icons on individual creativity, as well as showing that the very existence of extremely successful and highly visible individuals encourages people to strive to be "unique", to stand out from others, and to compete with the icons and the other people who try to emulate them. There are no controversies in the approach to this aspect of world creativity. According to the authors of this work, our entire society is deeply influenced by and constructed around widely shared icons. Icons shape common societal beliefs by enabling societies to establish dynamic norms and designing the behavior of members of society in a socially desirable way. They therefore influence how people represent themselves, either because they want to fit in with the rest of the society or because through their social representations and narratives they wish to differentiate themselves from others or to strive to become someone else and thus differentiate themselves from the rest of society.

We refer to the "icon effect" or the general effect of widely shared icons on society as societies' tendency to structure themselves according to people who have been most successful in a given field. As a result, fields of all kinds have relatively few people who dominate the attention. These people become famous as they get more and more widely shared attention and feedback, leading to more and more general visibility. We distinguish between individuals who are successful for specific groups of people and for larger groups of people. There appears to be a tendency to divide all famous people into "mainly male or mainly female" domains and, as we will show, the widespread influence exercised by these icons extends to various types of activities and performance.

9

Conclusion

Rise of the Icons: Although we are surrounded by such commanding presences, we rarely have a vocabulary for analyzing them. By focusing on a few vividly connoted icons, we have been able to show who they are or who they have been, some of the ways they have worked on us, and some of the ways in which, as Aristotle, Marx, and so many others believed, they reveal our world in forms more sharply defined than any other social science can give us.

The Effects of Fame: In so many ways, the world the icons have given us is tailored precisely to potentiality. It is not that mankind is significantly crueler or tenderer when Picasso and Rembrandt are looked upon in lonely grandeur than when such mere artists as Sickert or Balthus may request to be considered. It is rather that existing attitudes to art, humanity, or politics suddenly credit some sociopolitical set with the patterned significance currently profitable or notorious in Picasso, Marx, and company. If some of the ways in which we might sum up the effect of icons appear to be general, that is because the role of being amounts to the power of shaping symbols, in however transient a triumph, so as to allow the historically angular experience we mistake for self-evidence. Our work thereby calls attention to the remarkable intensity of the shaping done by icons, made up of those we have never known and of those we have only met in the shape that surrounds their clearinghouse character. They choose and confirm our world in the very credit we give their special experience of that world by which we live. The special intensity of this choice is the icon effect.